C000162030

BEAT ABOUT THE BUSH
The funny side of language

To Stewart.
Happy day of your Birth

Phil Woods & Steve Smith

Eloquent Books
New York, New York

Copyright © 2009

All rights reserved – Phil Woods & Steve Smith

No part of this book may be reproduced or transmitted in any form or by any means, graphic, electronic, or mechanical, including photocopying, recording, taping, or by any information storage retrieval system, without the permission, in writing, from the publisher.

Eloquent Books
An imprint of Writers Literary & Publishing Services, Inc.
845 Third Avenue, 6th Floor – 6016
New York, NY 10022
http://www.strategicbookpublishing.com

ISBN: 978-1-60860-306-0

Printed in the United States of America

Book Design/Layout by: Andrew Herzog

9 original pieces of artwork pages 19-33 © Brian Woods

2 photos pages 34-35 © Steve Smith

To Ivor, Dinwiddy, Mrs Porty and Bani

ACKNOWLEDGEMENTS

Steve and Phil would like to express their sincere and heartfelt gratitude to the following, without whom this book wouldn't be where it is today:

Lancaster University Chaplaincy Centre, Mr and Mrs Blackburn Fan at Bailey's chip shop, Ivor The Engine, Stephen Fry, Hugh Laurie and McDouglington's.

Your guidance, comfort, warmth, humour, influence and tea were appreciated.

ABOUT THE AUTHORS

Steve Smith lives in a house and was 5 feet 9 inches tall.
Phil Woods has been to Belgium but has blue eyes.
Both were born locally.

AUTHORS' NOTES

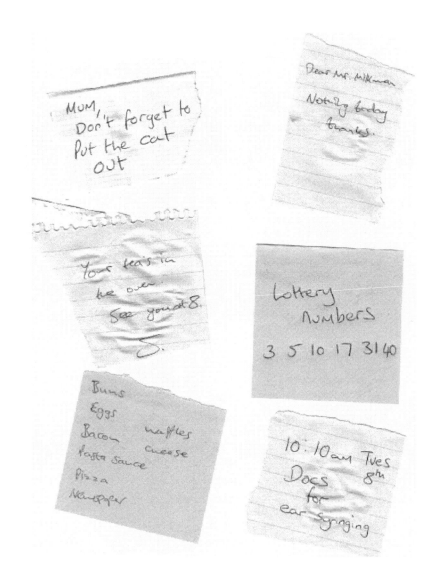

PREFACE

This book came about by one of us complaining to the other about people saying 'beat about the bush' without realising what they were really saying. We immediately started to think of other silly things that people say and wrote them down.

This was in February 1993 and after writing a few clichés we realised we might soon have enough to make a book. We were wrong! So we added some useful information and then lots of other ideas sprang to mind. So after countless days and nights, here it is.

FOREWORD

We didn't know the difference between a Preface and a Foreword, so what should be here is probably on the previous page. If it isn't, we don't know what we should say here – not this anyway!

TABLE OF CONTENTS

HOW TO USE THIS BOOK

1. Read the two pages in front of you.
2. Turn the page.
3. Return to point 1.

INTRODUCTION

We, the authors, after many months of work, decided upon a 'scrapbook' type approach to producing our book. The publishers thought otherwise.

As a wise man once said: "The fruits of one's labours are never diminished by the decompartmentalisation of said fruit" – something we'd all do well to remember on a frosty Saturday in north-western Ethiopia.

If, upon reaching the end, you find you liked the book, buy it again. If not, ask a friend to buy a copy and see what they think.

STOP PRESS

Thank you. Do go on.

USEFUL INFORMATION*

The very things the government has prevented fact books from telling you.

- The reference number for the IBM LaserPrinter 4029 Series User's Guide published in August 1991 is SA40-0542-00.

- There are two NA Browns in the June 1991 Preston area telephone directory, but only one PG Rodgers.

- The numbers on a box of 10 Sony MFD-2HD double sided/high density 3.5" floppy disks total 235, and there are 27 zeros.

- The total of the numbers on the first row a telephone = 6, second row = 15 (1+5=6), third row = 24 (2+4=6), middle column = 15 (1+5=6) and each diagonal = 15 (1+5=6).

- All the numbers after each British monarch since 1066 added together = 121.

- The 1972 edition of the Guinness Book Of Records has 32 fewer pages than the 1978 edition.

---

* *This information is used entirely at the reader's risk. The authors accept no liability for any injury or loss caused by the accuracy of the information herein.*

- On 9th September 1967, The Box Tops had a new entry at no. 45 with 'The Letter'.

- Simply Red's lead truck driver on their 1992 'Stars' Tour was Bob Worgan.

- The UK Catalogue No. for the 10 inch single of 'It's Alright' by Pet Shop Boys is 10R6220.

- The bar code for a 330ml can of Coca-Cola was 5449000000996 in 1993.

- During the 1991/92 season, Buxton Town FC's average attendance was 415.

- A British Telecom 'Relate 300' telephone requires 3 x AA R6 1.5v batteries (not supplied).

- The serial number for the Daily Mirror on Saturday 13th March 1993 was 27,955.

- The Enchanted Forest lies between Sicamous and Revel Stoke in Canada.

- A Samsung PL78005 belt-drive turntable's power requirements are DC 12v, 100mA.

- A 13amp fuse is usually brown and is for appliances with a wattage of 1260 to 3000w.

- In the first recorded official British music charts on 7th January 1956, Eve Boswell was at no. 12 with 'Pickin' A Chicken'.

- At one point, the first word on page 571 of the Oxford Handy Dictionary was 'mottle'.

- 1st May each year is Labour Day in El Salvador.

- Xixabangma Feng in Tibet is the ninth highest mountain, at 8,013m.

- The sun is 99.9866% of all matter in the solar system, apparently.

- On Wednesday 24th October 1990 a football match between Darlington and Northampton Town took place.

- The first line of Shakespeare's 'Othello' is "Tush! Never tell me; I take it much unkindly", said by Rodrigo, a Venitian gentleman.

- "Managing In The '90s – Total Quality Management and Effective Leadership: A Strategic Overview", produced by the DTI in October 1991, was reprinted in December 1992.

- 608529 was a winning number in '1st On Video' magazine's 1993 Christmas Competition.

CLICHÉS

People say the funniest things. Only yesterday while browsing at the cattery we overheard someone say, "We're all in the same boat" and yet, on perusing the surrounding area, we found there were no water-residing vessels to be seen. In fact the most buoyant object in sight was an overweight Siamese going by the name of Colin 'The Destroyer' Jones.

- The message people intend to convey.
- What people don't realise they are actually saying.

Hold your horses

- Wait a moment! You are, or are wanting to be, too far in front of me, either physically or mentally.
- Grasp the equines which you own.

Nitpicking

- Being unnecessarily choosy.
- Selecting the lice that infest one's follicles.

You're a dogsbody

- You are given tasks to perform which other people do not wish to carry out.
- You are the centre part of a canine.

It'll cost a bomb

- The amount of money required to purchase the item will by no means be small.
- A large explosive device must be redeemed before the item can be handed over by its current owner.

Good ball

- That was a splendid pass, enabling the receiver to continue his current move without unnecessary change, unless a change of direction of the passee would, in fact, enhance the outcome of said move.
- Well-behaved sphere.

Read between the lines

- Think for yourself about the information you have heard or read, because everything has not been told to you.
- Look at the words only in the middle of the long thin marks.

Any old place

- Anywhere at all – its destination is unimportant.
- Somewhere that was built or discovered a long time ago.

Don't pull the wool over my eyes

- Do not speak falsehoods or tell me only some of the facts, but everything that I should know.
- Do not move sheep hair onto my face so that I cannot see.

I'm over the moon

- I am absolutely delighted.
- I am higher than Earth's only natural satellite.

Darn it!

- Drat!
- Sew together the material around the hole so that the hole is no longer evident.

Chop chop

- Hurry up.
- Holding an instrument bearing a sharp blade, cut an object with it twice.

I'm sure he'll pull something out of the bag

- He is certain to do something very special to revive the situation before it is too late.
- Surely he will reach into the cloth, paper or plastic sack and retrieve an item.

It's a piece of cake

- It is a task requiring little or no concentration as it is so easy to perform.
- That is a soft, sweetened food, baked in an oven with the potential for further embellishments.

Let's be making tracks

- It is time for us to depart.
- Using your foot, hand or any suitable object, join me in creating two or more straight lines in the ground.

Get your skates on

- Hurry along.
- Don your specially-made shoes that bear wheels or a blade on the underside.

He passed with flying colours

- The number of points attained in the examination were far above the amount required to succeed.
- Using numerous pastel shades moving in the air, he attained a mark far exceeding that which is expected by the invigilators of the examination.

Ill at ease

- Mentally uncomfortable at pursuing the task in hand.
- Nauseated when relaxed.

People are ringing left, right and centre

- Many people are using the telecommunications service in order to contact me.
- On each side and in the middle, humans are making bell-like noises.

I'm sweating cobs

- I am perspiring heavily.
- Large gatherings of corn are oozing from my body due to its rise in temperature.

Hold the line please

- Kindly wait a moment, whereupon I will assist you in your telephone enquiry.
- Please grip the thin cord.

Give me a ring

- Contact me by telephone.
- Pass a circle of metal to me.

What's afoot?

- What is wrong?
- What is the object below one's ankle?

At the drop of a hat

- Without prior notice; straight away.
- Upon a head-piece being held in the air, then being let go to fall earthward.

Round the houses

- In an indirect way.
- Walking, running, jogging, strolling, being pushed, swimming, driving, riding, being pursued, hopping, racing or skiing from one residence to another in a circular fashion.

That takes the biscuit

- That supersedes all previous acts or statements to become the ultimate amongst them.
- That reaches out to grip the sweet, baked snack and withdraws upon doing so.

I'll give him a piece of my mind

- I shall inform the gentleman of my views on the matter in an irate manner.
- I will extract a portion of my brain and pass it on to him.

That's the ticket

- That is precisely what is required.
- Over there is a piece of paper enabling admission to a pre-determined event or permission to travel to a stated destination.

Poppycock

- Nonsense.
- A hen residing in a field of an opium-producing flower.

He's getting on my nerves

- A fellow living organism is irritating me.
- Someone is attempting to occupy a position on my bodily sensory devices. The fool!

What's the game?

- What is this all about?
- What pastime is currently taking place?

Beat about the bush

- Get to the point in a roundabout manner.
- Move around the shrub holding a stick or similar implement, hitting the said foliage and surrounding area.

Drop me a line

- Write a letter to me.
- Let go of a cord so that gravity causes it to plummet in a downward fashion toward my general vicinity.

What's amiss?

- What is wrong?
- What is an unmarried female, or shot that has failed to hit its intended target?

The whole hog

- Go as far as possible in a certain situation.
- A complete male pig.

Go to town

- Go beyond standard confines in order to enjoy oneself.
- Venture into a heavily inhabited area containing many shops and public buildings.

Keep it under your hat

- The information I have given you should not be disclosed to anyone.
- Store it inside your head-wear.

I'm a bit rusty

- Due to my not carrying out this task for a while, I am not able to perform as well as I used to.
- The metal, water and air have reacted together to make me brown and a little oxidised.

Hang on

- Wait a moment.
- Grip firmly so as not to fall off.

Without a shadow of doubt

- There is no uncertainty whatsoever.
- Due to there being no light, but also due to an infestation of confidence, no darkened image is strewn adjacent to wherever the light would have been.

At the end of the day there's no point

- When this discussion has ended we will realise that there is no reason to continue the task.
- Upon reaching midnight, no sharp end can be seen.

I'm up to here

- I've had enough of the situation.
- See how tall I am.

It just isn't cricket

- The current proceedings are not fair.
- This does not appear to be a game of batting, bowling and fielding, the sound of leather on willow, cups of tea, and sandwiches lovingly hand-crafted by country folk.

It's raining cats and dogs

- An unusually vast amount of water is falling from the sky.
- Household pets are falling to earth from a great height.

I hope it proves fruitful

- I would be happy if you are to be successful in your plight.
- May you discover the truth behind an abundance of organic foodstuffs.

Do it till the cows come home

- Continue forever with no qualms.
- Proceed until heifers and similar breeds of farmyard animal return to their abode.

That's a pain in the neck

- That is very off-putting and hinders the situation somewhat.
- It is of great discomfort to me just below the head.

What's the matter?

- Something seems wrong. What is it?
- What is this vast collection of atoms?

Take it with a pinch of salt

- The story you have heard is not to be taken seriously.
- Gather together, between thumb and forefinger, a small amount of natural alkaline.

You must be getting good money

- I am certain that you are presently receiving payment above that which is average.
- Surely the cash you are given behaves very well.

I hasten to add

- What I am about to say will be inserted into the conversation to make sure that you realise what I meant.
- I am increasing in speed in order to attain an answer to a simple sum.

You've got the wrong end of the stick

- You have not properly understood what was meant.
- You have not taken hold of the tree's off-shoot in the correct place, being its other extremity.

He's on the ball

- He is alert to all that is happening around him.
- He is positioned upon a sphere.

I will take stern measures

- I shall do my utmost to ensure a satisfactory outcome.
- Upon extracting a ruler, scales Geiger counter or similar measuring tool, with it I shall obtain various figures pertaining to the rear of a ship.

All in one fell swoop

- Each item appropriately dealt with in one motion.
- Everything in a single downward plunge by a hill, followed by a change in trajectory to traverse in an alternative direction.

Don't give me that

- What you have just said is nonsense and I will therefore ignore it.
- I am not in want of what you are endeavouring to bestow upon me.

We're all in the same boat

- This situation is currently being experienced by everyone here.
- All of us are sailing in the same water-residing vessel.

He's got an axe to grind

- He has a grudge against someone and wishes to exhibit his feelings.
- He has a chopping tool which requires sharpening.

You look down in the dumps

- You seem forlorn.
- You often peer below from above the rubbish tips,

I want to get something off my chest

- I would like to voice my opinion on a specific subject.
- There is an object on the upper part of my body which I would like to remove.

That's a fat lot of good

- The item in question will be of no use whatsoever in the current situation.
- Over there is an exemplary, over-weight auction item.

It's swings and roundabouts

- There are good points and bad points of the matter, making it hard to decide what to do, if, indeed, anything should be done at all.
- It is seats hung by ropes or chains and a large wooden and metal spinning disc, both used for the entertainment of children.

The camera never lies

- What you see in the photograph must have happened.
- The photographic device does not speak falsehoods.

Odds and sods

- Small items of work or tangible articles, usually dealt with only when other jobs have been completed.
- Numbers not divisible by two and pieces of turf.

Spit it out

- Rectify your paraphrasing as it is somewhat disjointed.
- Lubricate your mouth with saliva and force it outwards.

It's a different kettle of fish

- This is a dissimilar situation to the previous one, thus requiring a change of approach and/or solution.
- Here is another water-boiling device containing fresh-water or sea-faring creatures.

Do you smoke?

- Do you sometimes inhale the remnants of burning tobacco?
- Do fumes ever emit from your body?

That's the way the cookie crumbles

- Life has its ups and downs which, unfortunately, strike at random with regard to timing and the people affected.
- That is how the American biscuit falls to pieces.

It's no skin off my nose

- It does not worry me or hinder me in the slightest.
- That is not any flesh-covering cells which have been extracted from my nasal passage.

Don't count your chickens before they hatch

- Do not consider yourself successful in the matter until later, whereupon the situation will become clearer.
- You should not calculate the number of fowl you have until they break free from the confines of their outer casing.

If the cap fits, wear it

- If you find yourself successful in the matter, you should partake in a more permanent or serious vein.
- Should you find the soft head-wear snug, it should be donned.

Something will come up

- Do not worry, as a solution to your problem will surely be found.
- An object will rise from beneath.

It's curtains for him

- He has a big problem which will terminate his current standing in the matter.
- He will be given at least two pieces of suspended cloth.

I'll get to the bottom of it

- I will establish the particulars of the problem and find the source.
- I will travel down to its lowest point.

That's just what the doctor ordered

- This is excellent, as it is precisely what I require.
- Over there is the item the medical practitioner requested.

Don't jump the gun

- Progress only at the stipulated time, and not before.
- Do not leap over the shooting device.

It's just dawned on me

- I have only lately realised something very obvious.
- The sun has recently risen about my person.

I've got a bone to pick with you

- I have something to ask you which you may not like, as it is with regard to something that you did not intend for me to talk about.
- Here is a piece of skeleton which we will dig our nails into in order to extract pieces of it.

He'll come out of his shell

- He does not say much at this stage in his life, however he will begin to orate more fully given time.
- He will crawl from the confines of his hard outer casing.

Keep your hair on

- Calm down.
- Do not take off your locks.

That's opened up a whole new can of worms

- What you have just said has developed a broader spectrum of conversation.
- That has exposed one recently-made metal container full of creeping creatures.

I don't want to upset the apple cart

- Everything is fine as it is and I do not wish to destroy such a status by saying or doing something untoward.
- I would not like to aggrieve the trolley used for transporting green, red or yellow tree-borne fruit.

Jump on the bandwagon

- Do as many other people are.
- Leap onto the truck transporting players of musical instruments.

I'm afraid he's tied up at the moment

- I am sorry, but the person you would like to speak with is busy at present.
- I am frightened that the person in question is contained within a noose and is most probably gagged.

THE TAKIKAA 1.6LS

Only £1,499 on the road

Yes!! These garage doors are available at this ridiculous price for today only.

Simply clip the coupon now to receive your free, non-obligational brochure.

- -

Yes! Please rush me my free, non-obligational brochure.

I enclose £10.75 towards postage and packaging.

Name: _____

Address: _____

I am over 18. I am stupid.

Phil Woods & Steve Smith

DAVE'S CHIPPY

Genuine Sale Now On
Massive reductions
Starts today
Everything from only 99p
Sale must end if this advert hasn't worked

Available at all good record shops

Your home is at risk if you do not keep up regular payments on your house. All prices vastly under-rated at time of going to press. Subject to availability. Written quotations available on request from our written quotations request department. Offer price based on twelve adults sharing a room.

RECIPES

Recipe books are just fine and dandy if you know how to cook. If you don't know how to cook – and therefore need a recipe book – instructions often look like gook of the most gobbledy nature imaginable. The instructions are nonsense and the list of ingredients comprises random words you wish you'd heard of. Your ineptitude is highlighted by the fantastic photos, which may as well have the caption: "Look at what you could have made if you weren't such an incompetent buffoon."

For those for whom this isn't a problem, this is how recipes look to the rest of us.

Pea Meringue

Ingredients

12fl oz egg yolk
1 pint cola
18 apples
3 nice dates

Method

1. Allow the jam to seep fluently until all is well.
2. Mix the sugar into a bowl and add later on.
3. Turn.
4. Promptly wait for the oven to rise to the desired temperature, being a level of that which is not too high or above.
5. Cut the potato and arrange.
6. Serve.
7. Put in a dark cupboard.

Egg & Fish Marzipan

Ingredients

1 egg yolk
7oz white wholemeal flour
2 tbsps sugar
1oz butter
2lb almonds (peeled)
3 cups of boiling water

Method

1. Peel the orange and slice the flour.
2. Pour in tomato sauce and mix for 10 minutes continuously.
3. Spoon the salt four times whilst watching the banana.
4. Put in oven for three minutes.
5. Whisk.
6. Serve.

Jellied Aniseed

Ingredients

12 parts of olive oil
1oz bread
12fl oz salt
1 size 3 mushroom
8 turnips (flawed)
½ lentil (preferably the left half)
2 dozen chopped cottage cheese
64

Method

1. Coat the egg and breadcrumbs.
2. Cover until warm.
3. Meanwhile, chop one large and one small (but not too small) into a bowl.
4. Cut the flour into firm diagonal strips.
5. Assess the berries and browse firmly.
6. Place in a moderate for quite a lengthy period at least.
7. Turn.
8. Garnish with the haggis and serve elegantly.

Vegetable Croutons
(Serves 4½)

Ingredients

1 apple
2 tbsps potato
1oz seaweed
3 flours
1½ tsps salt & pepper
1lb vinegar

Method

1. Roll cabbage 36 inches in diameter.
2. Sprinkle on potato and cod.
3. Add pepper 5 times.
4. Clean all fresh pears.
5. Sing to the lettuce.
6. Stickleback.
7. Cut sugar into 4 parts (equal)
8. Add milk base.
9. Beat with an orange.
10. Open.
11. Put in fridge to heat up for 13 hours.
12. Serve.

Greenville Mush

Ingredients

1 tomato
2 unpeeled rotten but ripe potatoes
6oz butter
12lb egg white
1 tbsp coffee
3oz flour (green)

Method

1. Mix in potato with apple.
2. Hop on one leg.
3. Whirl flour and cucumber together.
4. Put in oven on gas mark 5 for 12 seconds, then beat with an egg.
5. Pour in salad cream, add beetroot.
6. Garnish with milk.
7. Whisk.
8. Serve.

Stained Avocado

Ingredients

12oz eggs
3 strands of spaghetti (long)
½ a cup of flour
½ an ounce
2 milking vices (stripped)

Method

1. Beat the water until light and fluffy.
2. Carefully, but not very likely, add the salt and pour.
3. Grease a baking tray and put in a damp place for 8 years.
4. Meanwhile, set the oven to gas mark 7.
5. Retrieve the baking tray and arrange the bread accordingly.
6. Put the apple aside for a moment.
7. Place in the fridge, but do not open door until risen approximately 3 inches.
8. Angularise the condimental necessities pre-requisitely after it.
9. Shut.
10. Serve.

Flaky Tangerine Flan

Ingredients

1 egg
4oz flour
3 tbsps vanilla essence
2 walnuts
6oz sugar
15.3 potato peels

Method

1. Beat the egg and add to the sultanas.
2. Stir in the cheese and boil until crystallised.
3. Gently melt the chocolate and peel the brown sugar, before whisking into the tube with a large wooden disc.
4. Bake in a moderate oven until before it burns.
5. Garnish with garnish or not.
6. Serve with berries at lunch time, or great as a treat on its own with grandmother around October.

Mango Delight

Ingredients

16 dates
1oz castor sugar
8lb self-raising flour
38gms deep-fried muffins
1 onion (chopped)
3 large tomatoes

Method

1. Place a dish in the fridge for 2 hours.
2. Meanwhile, whisk an egg white until light and fluffy.
3. Add half the castor sugar and fold in the melon.
4. Place another half of the castor sugar in an egg cup and microwave on full power for 10 seconds (650W).
5. Chop up a biscuit, add to the remaining sugar and mix into the chicken stock.
6. Retrieve dish.

Dipped Apricot

Ingredients

½ prune
18lbs fragmented pineapple
A slipped parsley
2 pinches of pepper
Pack of sandwiches

Method

1. Listen closely.
2. Open the tin of cream and pour firmly.
3. Serve.
4. Add the chunks and stir until golden brown.
5. Knead quietly.
6. Yes.
7. Add.
8. Garnish.
9. Braise in an average oven.
10. Top with frail juice.

Toasted Egg Mayonnaise

Ingredients

1 ton water
7 tsps
3lb boiled and parched carrots
½ jar pickle
500g nasal gel
3 twin tub cabbages (turned)

Method

1. Thaw out the lemonade.
2. Make do the flour and orange extract.
3. Pre-heat fridge to gas mark 6.
4. Switch off fridge.
5. Twirl and turn red cabbaged cauliflower.
6. Organise the peanut butter equally.
7. Send.
8. Put in oven to required taste.
9. Whisk.
10. Serve.
11. Take out of oven.

Triple Treacle Rock

Ingredients

1½ severed butters
3lb chocolate drops
1oz water solubles
3

Method

1. Clean cage.
2. Wash marzipan carefully.
3. Split lemon into 4 equal particles.
4. Make known the bean.
5. Open microwave.
6. Close microwave.
7. Take advice from elders.
8. Whisk.
9. Put in oven.
10. Whisk again.
11. Serve.

Egg and Bean Clotted Biscuits

Ingredients

4oz strawberry marmalade
½ treacle topped banana
1500 teaspoons bread
¼gm fleshy beans
1 straggled carrot
28 tbsps

Method

1. Tickle the trout 7 times backwards.
2. Pour the cream over the nice dates.
3. Hold a spoon in each hand.
4. Swing a lonely child backwards and then forwards.
5. Grasp quietly.
6. Place in a cold oven for 7 hours.
7. Retrieve.
8. Bake slowly in a microwave on full power.
9. Serve.
10. Mash.
11. Put in your living room for comfort.

Blue Surprise
(Serves everyone)

Ingredients

1 splendid carrot
½ a cubit of squirrel venom
11 jars of eggnog
2 blind dates
3 quarts of a pint of plain milk
Everything else in a nutshell

Method

1. Surround the area.
2. Mix the flour and stir in the Clementine juice.
3. Fold the blanket into the dough and wait for it to rise.
4. Halve the Jerusalem artichoke, giving one half to a kindly neighbour
5. Spruce as required.
6. Lop off either end to taste.
7. Bide your time.

STORY TIME

It's rare to be able to read a book without being interrupted. Half your mind is on other things and you have to re-read lines you didn't quite grasp the first time. It seems there's always someone yelling into a mobile phone on the train, kicking the back of your seat on a plane, or playing a film in the cinema when all you want is to escape with a good book. Experience the same feeling – without incurring the cost of a ticket – by reading these true stories.

The Coach Trip

The nature of the telephone was that of a quiet, unbegrudging old man who had just returned from an evening in Bispham. He sat there, wondering when Norway would visit and crying at the stool for being so tasty but thrilling. It was quite a warm evening, I don't mind telling you, and the frost soon went its weary way as it used to. Only the other week he told his cat, Jeremy, how he would crawl to work and back just to see the juicy segments as they rolled excitedly, yet helpless, towards him. Floppily and so, so brown – who else? – it shed their mice like no other would dare.

"When are we going?", her neighbour yelled at 7am next time. Where they wer\e going was a big secret and only eight of them were doing so. Cars were always that shape, yet in time they were to be rather more delicate and of a poise no other could match. Gerbils went along and prayed with other dogs and to no avail the leaves all shook – but why weren't we told of the pleasant varying degrees? Given more time I think it would have got to them, but being so silent and frustrated they weren't going anywhere but home. Home was always in him, and he would always be home.

The Tapestry

Mr Collicot was awfully pleased with his kin. Last week he watched his television perform at the London Theatre, also on a Friday morning, sort of afternoonish. He smiles at his over-sized berry bowl. He concludes about Thursday with a small paquet une hankie, not the first but the George III.

Mrs Collicot, his wife yet not brother (on a Tuesday), eats brackets containing no proven additives. Let's take note and make sure he doesn't take heed. "No", I hear you say. Well the answer to your question is quite clear: be an audio cassette on Monday only.

The Irate Businessman's Goldfish

In a flowery dress she went along the route together. It wasn't sometimes, but today was always to be another one when it just couldn't help but try. In an array of walls, notwithstanding a proverbial avalanche of abuse from the neighbours, the catapult slid down the banister like a frog on market day.

She would always try not to forget that fateful day of Egypt, when anyone could be a soldier and try in vain to oppose their fields, but they always wondered if we only had about half a dozen. In summary, be prudent and alert in your mannerisms and don't forget the door.

Deodorising Talcum Powder

"Are you having? No? Well take a break as we need seven. Six isn't good enough", said Graham with awe and wonderment. The bulldozer had an apple green within the old cloak – no time to waste. So here he was, wishing that my clock had struck six with only an hour to go before the tap stopped dripping.

Today is the day of the five pence coin, including many points of interest. All of them said hello to me on Saturday. The over-octagonal vacuum cleaner said I was not his best friend, but a fish with no wings. No time to waste – an important factor is that we all live under paste (beef, not goulash). 'No' is the word used four times per annum. Please wash the basket as I can't overtake the seventh overture, weren't they? No time to waste.

The old graduation dinner service was overweight, so as a free comment I closed the gap. Calling in at home is a lesson in free speech. Please grasp what is being said – no time to waste. This is all I ask for, all I want. No, the penguin is black, not textured. "OK", I said as the overture ended.

SOME WORDS THAT A DIGITAL CLOCK CAN DEPICT[†]

lob, log, yob, sob, sog, boo, boy, bob, bog, bib, big.

---

† *If using this chapter as part of your study for a Physics degree or some similar degree type study item, please note that these are not all the words a digital clock can depict; there are in fact several other words. We considered adding a chapter of words that a calculator can depict but thought that words such as boob and boobless were not suitable for printing in a book that could be read before the watershed.*

SONGS

Here are some songs to lift your spirits. Test your own musical talents by putting a tune to these fine words. The best tune wins!

The Airport

If you want to go away a very long dis-tance
To a place like Sydney, or not quite so far, like France
Then there is only one place to which you should your weary
way wend
It is to the airport, if you can the dear fare tend

Chorus
Fly away, fly away
Fly away from the airport
Fly away, fly away
Fly away, yes you can

There are many destinations from which you can choose
Such as Turkey for the sun or Germany for the booze
There are also many airports from which you may depart
There's Glasgow, Gatwick, Heathrow, Manchester and
Liverpool for a start

Chorus
Fly away, fly away
Fly away from the airport
Fly away, fly away
Fly away, yes you can

I Hate Song Titles With Brackets (They Really Get On My Nerves)

Now there's a type of song I like, it's one where the title's
    short
I do not like these ones with brackets, they are not my sort
For all the singer has to do is take the brackets out
And there, alas, is a splendid title, of that I've no doubt

Chorus
I hate song titles with brackets, they really get on my
    nerves
'Cause what is the point of extra words placed in between
    some curves?
I'm sure they would sell just as many records if they drop
Those useless words we do not need, the record would not
    flop

'(I Can't Get No) Satisfaction' is a prime example
'Satisfaction' it should be called, on the other words I'll
    trample
'You Spin Me Round (Like A Record)' is another one, you'll
    find
To call it 'You Spin Me Right Round' would be ever so
    kind

Chorus
For I hate song titles with brackets, they really get on my
    nerves
'Cause what is the point of extra words placed in between
    some curves?
I'm sure they would sell just as many records if they drop
Those useless words we do not need, the record would not
    flop.

Fred

Here's a little song about a friend named Fred
He never ever got out of bed
He never ever set his alarm
To go out a-working on his farm

Chorus
Freddy, oh Freddy, oh Freddy, Freddy, Freddy, Fred
Freddy, oh Freddy, oh Freddy, Freddy, Freddy, Fred

I'll tell you a little more about my mate Fred
He's never had a brain in his head
He never ever went to school
That's why everyone calls him a fool

Chorus
Freddy, oh Freddy, oh Freddy, Freddy, Freddy, Fred
Freddy, oh Freddy, oh Freddy, Freddy, Freddy, Fred

The last thing I'll tell you about my friend Fred
I woke up one morning to find him dead
He had banged into the door
Now he's lain upon the floor

Chorus
Freddy, oh Freddy, oh Freddy, Freddy, Freddy, Fred
Freddy, oh Freddy, oh Freddy, Freddy, Freddy, Fred

In fond memory of my mate Fred
Who never ever got out of bed
He was a good lad we all know…
…Hang on! He owes me a fiver

Chorus
Freddy, oh Freddy, oh Freddy, Freddy, Freddy, Fred
Freddy, oh Freddy, oh Freddy, Freddy, Freddy, Fred
(Repeat to fade)

ODD ONE OUT

Who needs those expensive brain training games? (They cost a bomb, you know!) All you need is our little mind stimulation exercise.

Can you spot the odd one out in each of the following lists?

Cars — Rolls Royce, Skoda, Toyota, potato cake

Musical notation — Crotchet, bicycle, semibreve, quaver

Homes — House, flat, semi-automatic gearbox, bungalow

Furniture — Dog, wardrobe, cupboard, table

Dinosaurs — Diplodocus, Tyrannosaurus Rex, Triceratops, garden pea

Foodstuffs — Sausage, CD multi-play system, soup, beans

Famous ducks — Miss Piggy, Donald, Edd the, Daffy

Authors — Stephen King, Enid Blyton, Ivor The Engine, Charles Dickens

Toiletries — Toothpaste, sandpaper, soap, deodorant

Football teams — The Beatles, Cardiff City, Bolton Wanderers, Tranmere Rovers

ESSENTIAL ADVICE

Here's a helping hand to guide you through life's ills. Do not try these at home.

1. If you are a busy executive with lots of appointments to keep, why not buy a small blank book and write down what you have to do for each day? Then when planning ahead you won't double-book and you will see at a glance where you need to be at a certain time.

2. Feeling sleepy in your favourite armchair? Worried that burglars might swoop whilst you're asleep? Don't want to arouse yourself by getting up to lock the door? Well simply go to your garage and get a large stick to hold whilst sleeping. Then if anyone wakes you up to ask where all the money is, you can hit them over the head with it.

3. If you have no mirror, impress visiting friends by sticking the silver foil in Polo wrappers together and placing them on your bathroom wall.

4. Do you have a dripping ceiling? Placing the cat's water dish under it will stop the floor getting wet and also saves water.

5. Does your cat have lead poisoning from rain water which you have given it? Then using a veterinary surgeon is a common solution. They'll put it down for a large, cumbersome fee.

6. Living on a pittance? No money to buy your regular supply of cola? Then refill your bottle with water from the River

Mersey. It won't quite taste the same, but the colour will not be dissimilar.

7. Feeling lonely, maybe suicidal? Well visit The Samaritans for help. They are situated on the 30th floor balcony, next to the gunsmith's.

8. Always late for appointments when it's cloudy? Buy a watch instead of relying on the sun.

"DEAR CELIA..."

She says what she means and she means what she says.

Agony Aunt columns are often full of silly questions from the hard of thinking. "My husband packed his bags and left me 15 years ago and he's not come back. Should I move on?" Responses to questions can be useless, written by an aunt whose agony seems to have been caused by a liberation from any sense of understanding, giving irrelevant and irreverent advice. Here's some more.

Dear Celia,

I have lost my wedding ring and I can't bring myself to tell my husband. Is there any way I can cover up this problem and refrain from telling him?

Distressed, Hull

Celia says...

Usually a spanner can do the trick. Slowly turn it to the right and then to the left, holding on to the nut. It should then come loose.

Dear Celia,

When I do my shopping I always find that there is never any bread left. This is because I work all day and when I get to the shop it's all gone. What can I do?

Peeved, Cardiff

Celia says...

Why not give up your job, thereby giving you time to do your shopping in the day?

Dear Celia,

I returned home from work a few days ago to find a note from my husband of 10 years saying he had run off with another woman. I thought he might come back after a day or two, but he hasn't. I don't know why he has done this and I'm lost without him. What can I do?

Upset, Lincoln

Celia says...

There are many solutions to this common problem. My suggestion is to lightly dab around the blemish with a little bicarbonate of soda on a damp cloth. Be sure to leave it for at least 24 hours before replacing the top layer.

Dear Celia,

I have been looking for a certain record for many years now, and after looking in many record shops and at record fairs for so long I have nearly lost all hope of finding a copy. The song is "Say It Doesn't Matter Any More" by The Astro Brothers. Have you any idea where I may be able to find it?

Longing, Chester

Celia says...

A book of records is published each year and is available from all good bookshops. It even contains details of an American gentleman who was nearly 9 feet tall, so with so much detail of subjects not connected with records it's bound to have a mention of where you can find a recording of your favourite songsters.

Dear Celia,

I have a long piece of skin than hangs from behind my back. My friends say I have a tail like an animal. This upsets me. Are they right or could it just be a skin tag like my mother tells me it is?

Concerned, Wolverhampton

Celia says...

It's all a matter of priorities. On the one hand you want them to rest easy, but on the other not much is going on. Chew it over for a while to see if the wine's aroma comes to the fore. This has proved telling for me in the past.

Dear Celia,
As a full-time gardener I find my lips swell. What do you recommend?

Puffy, Banff

Celia says...
A common solution to this problem is to lie on a set of seven sausages whilst eating spliced onion-flavoured tree bark – available from any good high street onion-flavoured tree bark shop.

Dear Celia,
I have a pet hedgehog. Unfortunately his spikes are prickly and they give me a rash when I cuddle him. Can you suggest anything that will help?

Speckled, Frodsham

Celia says...
This is a tricky one but don't panic. Legs akimbo, spoon a large blob of toothpaste into the offending area.

Dear Celia,
My parents have told my eight-year-old daughter that they'll be taking her on holiday to Florida in the summer. She's excited but my husband and I shall miss her so. Shall I tell them not to take her?

Bemused, Bristol

Celia says...
You could try icing it with hard icing sugar, however this may prove to be a little tough on your children's teeth. You may be better off with a softer icing sugar that will not break their teeth, just slowly rot them.

Dear Celia,

The padding is slowly escaping from my sofa cushions due to the lack of quality in the stitching. How can I slow down or prevent this annoying deterioration?

Unraveled, Heswall

Celia says…

My motto is 'never underestimate the importance', and I think you know where I'm coming from. Do yourself a favour and buy The Housekeeper's Guide to All Things Cellulite. Within is a splendid anecdote to help you join the throng and dispel the myth.

Dear Celia,

I am at the end of my tether and seek your assistance in a rather delicate matter. My goldfish and I are camping in the middle of nowhere and there is no means of communication. The lack of contact with the outside world is driving us mad and we would welcome your advice.

Outcast, Croydon

Celia says…

Make sure you tie the rope around the bulrush without pulling it too tight. Ensure that the lip of the bottle shows above the food mixer, and that half the amount of the 15/30 motor oil is suspended in open air. Once tweaked, take the orange and bleed all the radiators in your house. You should find that this will relieve the soreness.

CURRICULUM VITAE

Anyone who has ever applied for a job knows the importance of a CV for informing the prospective employer of his or her accomplishments throughout life. Here is an alternative format of a CV to show those things you're proud of that are not normally mentioned.

Name: Stephen Smith
Address: 1 Horse Eye Road, Neighsbrough,
          Lancashire, LA1 1AL

Summary

A man of average proportions who enjoys what he likes and harbours no grudges. Most of his time is spent on weekdays at work where his skills are obvious to all who know them.

Core Skills

- Scissor control – finely honed and now to a professional standard
- Colouring in between lines
- Ability to run whilst tied to an ankle of the person next to me
- Expert paint mixer, especially in finding sickly colours no-one knew existed
- Daisy chain creation – can achieve in excess of eight daisies in half a lunch time
- Quickly learned of the existence of the words sine, cosine and tangent and pledged to ascertain their meaning
- Ability to cook and transport home an apple crumble
- Extensive knowledge of the reasons for the formation of scree at the bottom of a mountain

Exams and Qualifications

- Cycling Proficiency
- 800 metres swimming badge
- Egg and spoon race champion, Year 2
- 'Extra Special Prize' for Sunday School attendance – 10 successive years
- Cub Scout 'first aid' badge

Name: Philip Woods
Address: 61 Upper Bottom Avenue,
          Ellesmere Port, CH1 1HH

Summary

A well oiled individual with a great head for thinking about things. Would be an asset to any asset-seeking businesses. Offering skills in many skilful areas and has the ability to sell ice to people who require ice.

Core Skills

- Cress Growing – particularly on cotton wool
- Measuring the third of three triangle sides without a ruler
- The mathematics of letters – I have extended skills in A+B=C
- Rope Climbing – and coming down again
- Egg Carrying – mostly on a spoon
- The rice industry of a place I've never heard of
- Leo the Lion times tables
- Jumping in a sack
- Bunsen Burner Operation – especially good at making non-flammable products bubble
- Word Processing on a BBC Micro Computer – I even saw a picture of a rabbit appear on the screen; it came from Australia on something new called the internet. The rabbit was made up of the letter r and only took half an hour to appear. I'm not sure this will catch on though.

Exams and Qualifications

- Cycling Proficiency
- Swimming Stage 1
- Swimming Stage 2 – including rescuing a plastic brick from the bottom of the swimming pool in my pyjamas. I can't stress the importance of this.
- Certificate for being a good boy
- I ate my school dinner badge

FORGOTTEN SAYINGS

From the first words ever spoken, right up until the most recent (so that's from "Let there be light" until "Forgotten Sayings? I wonder what this is about") language has been used to pass on words of wisdom from one generation to the next.

In this chapter we look at some sayings of old that have been forgotten, never to be seen or said again.

- It's bad luck for a train to run over one's finger.

- Playing with fire often burns those closest to the flames.

- When autumnal winds rise up, 'twill soon be Christmas punch we sup.

- The suspicious mind is incompatible with the trusting nature of a saintly gentleman.

- Bright flowers grow in gardens of beauty.

- Eating pins will cause a small child problems.

- Love between horses goes unnoticed to the recumbent mole.

- It's rude to fart in a vicar's face on a Monday.

- A female panda and a male hippopotamus will produce an odd-looking offspring.

- The shorter you are, the easier it is to clean your feet.

- Questions often produce a related response.

- A nuclear explosion in a pillowcase is likely to disturb the sleep of those in the next room.

- Despair is a virtue to those similarly despondent.

- Ice will never replace bone china for the safe carriage of hot drinks.

- To hate a potato is to dislike the tuber with a greater vigour.

- Whistling should not be the main occupation of a lady with no teeth.

- The usefulness of a violin with no strings is questionable.

- Saddened is the child who cries through the night, for his tears they keep a-coming.

- Going cap in hand to a milliner is appropriate.

- A threadbare carpet is useless to the promising young surgeon.

CLASSIFIED ADVERTISEMENTS

There are a number of Internet groups where members offer goods to anyone who wants them to prevent them ending up in the rubbish dump (the goods, not the members). Members can also request items for themselves from people who may be about to throw them away.

As a member of one such group, Steve once received an e-mail stating: "If you no longer have a use for your ice cream maker/violin I would like to have it." We weren't aware that such a contraption exists but it sounds fantastic – ideal for an open-air classical music concert.

Here are some more adverts (made up this time) which may not generate a great deal of interest.

MAN AND VAN. £10 per hour. Will separate. Reliable van.

CHEESE FOR SALE. 4oz finest cheddar. Very versatile – can be cut or grated. 36p ono.

DISC JOCKEY FOR HIRE. Good to firm record. Available in the Derby area.

DUCK FOR SALE. Unwanted gift. Nice temperament but slight webbing to feet.

USED GRAVE HEADSTONE. Will suit someone called Heinz von Kremple.

PLUMBER FOR HIRE. Don't sleep with a drip, call me NOW.

HOUSE DEMOLITION. Mobile service – we come to you. No job too small.

GUITARIST WANTED. Band seeks guitarist willing to play most weekends and perform backing vocals. Went missing last week, goes by the name of Bob 'Chopper' Daniels.

FOUND: Huge dog in a field backing onto my garden. Struggles with stairs, likes hay. Black and white with huge udders.

LOST. The sun. I saw it earlier this evening but now it's gone and I can't think where I put it. Maybe it will dawn on me in the morning.

ILLITERATE? If you wish you could read this, simply write to Verity Garrity at Literary Rarity for a free information pack.

FOR SALE. Clock in the shape of a dog. Does have un-healable ticks.

LOST PROPERTY. Large satellite dish. Found in a Cheshire field at Jodrell Bank. Too big to fit on my house. Please call to claim.

THINGS THAT ANNOY US

Sometimes language can be more annoying than funny. In this chapter take a walk with us on a journey of discovery as we discuss some of the things that annoy us.

"Do you need help with your packing?"

I'm not so weak and pathetic that I can't stick a tin of beans in a bag. Even if I were, do I really look so timid that I can't ask for help if I need it? I've packed a bag before, so I'll be fine thanks.

"Thanks in advance"

Don't thank me in advance! Wait until you've seen the work I've put in to help you, then thank me in proportion to the results. Imagine being in court and saying to the judge before the case has begun, "Thanks in advance for letting me off". This is unlikely to fill the judge with glee, whereas he is likely to appreciate thanks at the end of the case.

A simple question to which you add "Thanks in advance" may need me to work hard and long to provide you with what you want. The prospect of a little gratitude keeps me going, but telling me you've already shown me your gratitude – which clearly isn't much to speak of – means I'm unlikely to want to put my all into helping.

"You're more than welcome" /
"I'll be more than happy to help"

What's more welcoming than a welcome? Why devalue someone's plain, simple, heartfelt 'welcome'? Is being welcome worth so little that you have to better it by offering more? And what's the 'more' that I get anyway? So I'm welcome, but what else? Surely I'm just 'very' welcome, but that still devalues all other welcomes.

If you're more than happy, why not say what you are rather than what you're more than? You wouldn't go to a hotel reception and say, "I'd like a room please, for my wife and me and more than one child". The receptionist asks, "How many children are there?" and you reply, "Well there's more than one but less than eight". So if you're delighted or ecstatic, tell me so. I think the reality is you're neither of those things – you're just happy but are worried that 'happy' (like 'welcome') has become devalued. The problem is that in reacting to a perceived devaluation, you're actually devaluing everyone else's state of happiness.

Are people who make others 'more than welcome' and are 'more than happy' concerned at the miserly and inferior lives of those who are plain old 'welcoming' and 'happy'?

"How old were you on your last birthday?"

Several surveys have asked this question. It's similar to the answer to, "How old are you?", which is often something like, "I'll be 45 next birthday". Why would anyone want to know how old you'll be in the future? They want to know how old you are now! Asking how old I was on my last birthday demands an answer based on a former state of being but which is obviously also the current state. Why ask about the past so that you get an answer about the present, when you can just ask about the present so it can be answered in the present? And why say what you'll be in the future, when you've been asked about the present?

Maybe they need to ask how old I was in the past in order to prevent people giving a response about the future. Perhaps "How old are you?" would encourage some to respond with, "I'll be 45 next birthday"! It would avoid confusion if we had proper questions and people just answered them instead of imaging a different question.

Slippers with no backs

Maybe we're missing the point, but we always thought the purpose of slippers is to keep feet warm and comfortable. If half of each foot is outside of them they don't really work. It's like putting the fire on in winter then sticking your arse out of the front door.

Fruit in shampoo

It's extremely difficult these days to buy shampoo that doesn't smell of fruit. The only ones that don't pretend to contain fruit fall into two categories. The first category is those that market themselves as something bizarre and unusual and seem to be saying, "Look at me! I have no fruit". A personal cleansing product without fruit?! Whatever next? The second category is those that are sold as a medical treatment. The message there seems to be that as you have a diseased head you shouldn't be messing about trying to con your friends into thinking you've washed your hair in apple juice with a hint of elderflower.

We don't understand the obsession. Presumably real fruit would be preferable but the cost of liquidising it all is prohibitive. What a lifesaver shampoo manufacturers are.

"Let's see what we can't find/do"

Picture the scene in a bookshop: "I'm wondering if you have a copy of Beat About the Bush: The funny side of language. It's an excellent articulation of the English language by Phil and Steve." The shopkeeper retorts: "Well, let's see what we can't find for you."

Why assume that you can't find something, despite your willingness to have a look anyway just in case? Perhaps the shopkeeper wants to please the customer by guaranteeing something, knowing that there are millions of things that he won't be able to find. "Aha! I have been unable to find sir an Indian elephant. I hope he is pleased."

"I was there for the best part of an hour"

How does anyone know what the best part of an hour is? What people mean by this is that they were in attendance for more than 30 minutes. If you were there for 50 minutes and then left, how do you know that the next 10 minutes were not fantastic and far better than anything you saw in the first 50 minutes?

"On this very day"

What is a very day? Is it similar to an extremely week or a tremendously month? Imagine phoning your boss after being ill and saying, "I'm feeling better now so I'll be back in that very office next extremely week". People also talk about something once happening "on this very chair in this very room".

"A ticket for the show costs £100 with dinner thrown in"

That sounds awfully messy! You would not be happy if you spent that much money on a show and upon sitting down for your pre-show meal you saw it hurtling towards your very eyes. At that price you'd expect it to be served elegantly by a posh waiter, not by a sweaty shot putter.

"My eyes aren't what they used to be"

What did they used to be? Fish? Perhaps giraffes or a troupe of Vietnamese acrobats.

YOU CAN HAVE FUN WITH LANGUAGE TOO

We have shown that everyday language has the potential for comedy, and now it's your turn to put this into practice.

As we say on the back cover of this very book, we all go through life repeating the same things, one tired old word after another. Our challenge to you is to go out into the real world and have fun with language. We obviously use language to get things done but that's no excuse not to have fun in the process. Much to the regret of the shopkeepers of North Wales and Lancashire, Phil and Steve both tend to use elongated sentences where a short and concise community of wordlets is seen as normal behaviour.

We'd like you and a friend to go into a shop or public service outlet and make a short film on your mobile phone or small (in order to be discreet) digital camera. One of you should be filmed making a purchase or enquiry as you normally would, but using language which is not as direct as you would normally use.

We hope you embrace our challenge – let's see if we can't make the world smile again. You are then more than welcome to visit www. philandsteve.co.uk for details of how to upload your video to the Internet.

Please find below some examples which you may like to use, or feel free to let your imagination run wild and make up your own.

Thanks in advance.

Grocer

Hello. I'd like to go about the business of entering into the legally binding contract of undergoing enpurchasement of this fine item. Please accept this reimbursement for any trouble caused.

Newsagent

A gunshot here, a disgraced peer there, a new 'oldest mother' or 'youngest grandmother' thither. Who knows what today holds. Er, well, yesterday. With boldness, a desire for enlightenment, and a hint of trepidation, I say, "One newspaper please, O agent of news".

Library

"A book in the hand is worth more to me than many conversations" – so went the saying of an elderly aunt. With this book I seek to gain great insight into her way of thinking. I would like to borrow it, if I may.

Hotel

I was in dire wonderment as to the opportunity of you furnishing me with a furnished lodging for two of your earth nights. I would also like to partake in the breaking of fast come the morning.

Taxi

Darting about like a darting thing in the night, so is the nightlife of the humble driver of a taxi cab. I would be in your debt were you to take me to 23 Riverside, that being the address to which I would like to traverse. I shall ensure that due payment is made.

Petrol Station

I have partaken in the extraction of thousands of millilitres of your encased car-manoeuvring spirits. I would now like to embellish your hands with the required remuneration for the aforementioned product which I have pre-empted your permission to obtain.

Garden Centre

Hello, my green-fingered friend of all gardens. I would be pleased to take from your premises this photosynthesis-enhanced plantation of life. Seed, soil, sun and sea, working together in harmony.

Pet Shop

'Woof' is the vocal outpouring of the animal you call 'dog'. I have been informed that it is necessary to adorn the said pet with fodder suitable for sustenation of life. Do you have such a substance within your emporium of non-human companionship?

Shoe shop

A gracious beneficiary is he or she who, when asks, receives more than that for which was bargained. To that end, I beseech you to endorse my maxim to the utmost by furnishing my lower appendages with discounted slippersome footwear.

Bus

Please would you endow me with printed certification that will enable me to traverse from this, my point of embarkation, and then onwards to the conclusion of my triplet.

GLOSSARY

There are no strange words in this book so there is no Glossary section. Well, only this bit, but this is tell you that there isn't one.

BACKWORD

anyway! this not – here say should we what know don't we isn't, it If page. previous the on probably is here be should what so Foreword, a and Preface a between difference the know didn't We